AF255876

Words

Poems of Life and Living

Poems of Love and Loss

Meditations in Verse

Shirley Koers

Words © Shirley Koers 2026

ISBN: 978-1-9234769-7-4 (paperback)

All rights reserved. No part of this publication may be reproduced, stored in a retrieval system, or transmitted in any form or by any means electronic, mechanical, photocopying, recording, or otherwise, without the prior written permission of the author.

Published in Australia by Shirley Koers and InHouse Publishing.
www.inhousepublishing.com.au

Printed in Australia by InHouse Print & Design.

A catalogue record for this book is available from the National Library of Australia

Foreword

I, Shirley Cecilia Freese Koers, was born on November 11, 1928 exactly ten years after World War One ended, and received all my education to university in India. Australia has been my home since April 25, 1970 (ANZAC DAY is my Australian birthday!), of which ten years were spent in New Zealand. I take this opportunity to wholeheartedly thank Australia for its incalculable gifts to me, especially of marvellous friends. God bless, preserve and prosper it forever. My two previous books are referred to in a footnote in this work.

About Judith

I am very grateful to dear friend Judith Akins who unexpectedly took an interest in this project and provided invaluable help. Given our great life differences, Judith a successful businesswoman and I a former teacher of senior English language, literature and history in Catholic secondary schools, our friendship is unusual to say the least. Perhaps I should share how it began. Before I moved into the retirement complex I now live in, I owned a duplex half in a small complex of which Judith became the body corporate manager. When I sold I wrote thanking her for the two meetings we had had with her. Three years later in 2017 I received an acknowledgment. She had misplaced my letter and was now thanking me. Well... I couldn't believe it. A woman who managed about 220 bodies corporate had taken the time and trouble to respond to my letter of appreciation, so I wrote back telling her she had blown my mind. All friendships begin mysteriously and there is often no telling how the seed is sown, especially between people of very different backgrounds. It is definitely heavensent, "a gift from the gods". One can only be exceedingly grateful to have a friend and be a friend.

Contents

You are writing a gospel
A chapter each day,
By deeds that you do,
By words that you say.
Men read what you write
Whether faulty or true.
Say, what is the gospel
According to you?

-- Author Unknown

Poems of Life and Living

"At the edge of the desert sands

roll the waves of blue water."

From the letter of a dear friend.

1. To Friends Then and Now

Of all the unsaid words that never can
Rise into speech,
You are the thoughts hovering beyond the span
Of fancy's reach.

You are the comfort of wrapt solitude
When stars are seen.
You are the wordless message understood
In heaven's dream.

You are the kindness Love itself bestows
On everyone,
Not accidental, but intended blessing
Never done.

You are the ideal almost sought in vain
A lifetime through,
You are the ideal found in spirit's pain
That nurtured you.

You are the time, the care, the thoughtfulness
Ever on-going.
You are the prize God-given at the goal
Of final knowing.

You are the goodness that will hold in thrall
My paltry verse,
You are the dearest friends most loved in all
The universe.

In this 1974 poem I tried to capture a recurring childhood dream and, interestingly, once while listening to a radio programme on Dreams, a caller rang and described a dream identical to mine. To this day I regret not following up the matter, at least for her sake.

2. My Dreaming Dream

I dreamed a dream when I was little,
A dream of mystery.
I saw a tree all bare and brittle
Growing in a sandy sea.
No touch of green relieved its branches,
Its beauty was its bareness,
And standing in its silver sand
It challenged my awareness.
I'd stand for hours in many dreams
Beneath my lonely tree,
Fling my arms wide and let the sand
Run through my fingers, free.
But as it did so it would turn
Into the coarsest gravel.
No plea of mine could hold it back,
No thought my dream unravel.

I grew up and dreamed no more
This dream of childhood years,
But all I reached for fled before
My longing and my tears.
Now I have found the meaning locked
Within this memory,
"A grain of wheat must die to live.
I have a plan for thee."

Shirley Koers

Our resurrection is begun
Upon this Earth, it's said.
However long the race to run
This is the path to tread.

3. The Might of Words -- a Sonnet

A hurried line can transport to a home
The thrilling wonder of a new-born fame.
The judge pronounced: mere words. The youthful head
Droops blanched and cold. Just words in whispered tone
Win man a mate, create or smash a name.
A magic word and yearning hearts are fed.
Plain words life's many barriers can surmount,
One word outweighs and cancels sin's account.

Mere words today like blades went through my breast.
Why should I care? Why must tears scald my eyes?
Why bear the blood-hue on my cheeks? Go rest.
The spoken words though they be demon lies
Are not so deadly as what goes unsaid.
These timely drops of bitterness are bread.

One of my earliest poems referring to the difficulties experienced during my Senior Cambridge (overseas examination) year, 1946, as a schoolgirl in British India.
A sonnet is a 14-line poem of five feet in a line with a weak-strong, weak-strong beat: Thĕse tíme/lў dróps/ôf bít/tĕrnéss/aře bŕead."
This metre is called iambic pentametre. It is the metre in which William Shakespeare wrote all his 37 plays and his Sonnets and Poems. A sonnet has a special rhyme-scheme: usually abba, abba, cde, cde; or cd, cd, cd. Mine is a bit different.

Shirley Koers

4. A Sonnet For Our Seniors

They will go out now free, into the great
Mysterious world, half understood, half known,
The world of harvests reaped from harvests sown,
And like Macbeth will "take a bond of fate".
Their many hopes run high, but they must wait
Until the dreams they dream mature have grown
And they have made their selves their very own.
For loss of that, what gift can compensate?

They are so young, yet deeply are aware
Of all life's promise, all the love it holds.
Not to receive, but to bestow, because they care
And in their patience to possess their souls.
And so they go, but they will not forget
The "learning years", when high ideals were set.

Written for 71 girls in Grade 12, November 1, 1970 when I was teaching at
Lourdes Hill College, Hawthorne, Brisbane, Queensland, Australia.

5. Himálayas - My Mountain World

Oh how I miss my mountain land
on the roof of the world by Everest's knees!
Oh how I long to visit again,
with the scent of the pine on the evening breeze!

Give me again
the little train
that climbs the heights at nine thousand feet,
give me the sunsets,
give me the rain
and the people in a Himálayan retreat!

I love a hill, I love it high,
its beauty stark against the sky.
I'd love to reach the sunset peak
and chase a cloud and hear the bleak
whine of the wind, angry and loud
blowing away my sunlit cloud.

Your sunburnt strand I see no more,
Once-lovely dreams are fading fast.
But I shall find you, mystic land,
I shall come back to you at last.
The cross I wear shall mingle in prayer
with the Buddhist flags waving high in the air
and the prayer wheels turning
and the lonely heart's yearning
shall cry to the Lord in the mountains there.

Shirley Koers

Oh let me climb,
take me up high
and on a mountain let me die
like Moses in the long ago!

Could anyone loving a mountain be fettered
even behind iron bars being bettered?
Leave me forever to my love.
And you, my friend, go back below
Himálaya, Abode of Snow,
and tell the world the die is cast,
the ageless hills are mine at last.

1971 -- Written in Brisbane, Australia, a year after leaving India. I was actually
too overworked to be homesick!

6. Twentieth Century Boast

Not sewing machines and typewriters,
Not aeroplanes and motorbikers,
Not all the possibilities of steam,
Not all that atom tests may mean;
Not telephones and cable wires
And skyscrapers and church spires,
Not all the gadgets of a factory plant,
To every one of these Avaunt!

Not even genius in the television --
We now have AIs as the new invention!
Not even church rank, Cardinal Feretti,
It's the girl-saint, Mária Goretti.
That even in the Twentieth Century
A girl could die to save her chastity!
Again a saint has shown the holier way,
The stuff God's friends are made of in our day.

Born in Italy 1890. Died 1902 aged 12.
1 First syllable of the name stressed to keep the five-foot weak-strong beat.

Shirley Koers

7. Christmas in Memoriam

Remembering Child Murder Victim Jamie Bulger

Little boy done to cruel death,
Little boy murdered lying cold,
Little Christ figure sacrificed,
The Herod who killed you ten years old.

Holy Innocent, wounded, bleeding,
Society cries in righteous shame.
But oh, while tender flesh is pleading
Let one and all take some of the blame.

For we have fed young people poison.
By not teaching love we have fostered hate,
We have glorified violence, lust, aggression,
And withered fruits are wept too late.

Too late for two-year-old Jamie Bulger?
Say not such death is ever in vain.
The Risen Christ begins restoration:
Abundant life from abundant pain.

The tragic case in England of two young children killing a toddler

8. An Answer

This morning
things being without that 'spark from heaven'
and my spirits trapped
in terrible gloom,
I said to God, CONVINCE me.
Convince me that you NEED me.
ME.
My little contribution...
My special gifts...
What IDEA would you wrap in a person like me?
Tell me.
I couldn't think of one.

Then the knock sounded.
Two Mormons,
Americans and very young
stood there expectantly.
Come in, I smiled, mustering my Christian love.
We shared.
Not their message or mine,
just Jesus, as I wished,
Val, Edward and Shirley,
forgetting their differences.
Then my dear,
you also came, it was princely.
"God's Gentle Rocket" I dub thee Sir Knight/Lady!
God, you need me all right.

19 December 1979 - New Zealand, the year following my husband Jack's death.

9. A Prayer for Kampuchea

When Cambodia was under the Khmer Rouge

Lord of the Universe
receive them now into land of lapis lazuli,
their pagoda paradise.
You wouldn't let their sufferings 'merit' less,
Lacking formal introduction
to the Saving Name.
When on that heap of straw
and on that Tree
you loved me -- no strings attached --
you won all humanity.

Cambodia the Beautiful,
"Rice Bowl of Asia",
exotic unbartered pearl of gentleness, and courtesy,
alas now your limpid eyes
reflect horrors past telling:
butcherings and drownings, mass murders, malnutrition,
your rice growing bitter, your children lying broken.
A civilised Peace Prize
crowns the YEAR ZERO
while the tears of the Buddha
dissolve like the rainbow.

Lord of the Universe
receive me too.
Amid our great plenty
let us recognise you.

1979 Napier, New Zealand, REFUGEE DAY

10. Transfigured Light

You were a stranger once to me.
I admired your ways and your preaching was "great",
The depth of your thought, so simply expressed,
Said a lot to my mind to which I could relate.

But I did not know you till you lifted the veil
That gave me to see you were human too,
And spoke to my heart of the light that had died,
And the Jesus in me met the Jesus in you.

Now the words of Scripture are being fulfilled
Of the "beautiful feet" that carry his name,
That answer the need and follow the call
And think only of giving and not of the pain.

What a glory it is to live by Faith
No matter how long the soul's "Dark Night".
Awaiting at last is the Vision of God
In the glory of his unending Light.

For a priest for whom while still in the Seminary "The light suddenly went out of my life and never came back." His superiors decided nevertheless to ordain him and throughout the ceremony' "I wept with joy and gratitude." Life in the Spirit seminar, November 1978, a month after Jack's death.

Shirley Koers

11. Old Nuns

Gems are buried in caves of earth
And treasures unknown in the depths of the sea
But in the heart of the faithful spouse
Who can total the wealth amassed for thee?

Her feet have ached and her hands have toiled,
Her working hours were oppressed with care,
But she gave unstintingly of her best
And when you called, Lord, she was there.

In cheerful service now grown old
She still remains on the battle scene,
Singing the song that filled her heart
When her tree of life was fresh and green.

Is there a more beautiful thing in the world
Than a wrinkled nun whose hair is white,
Whose voice is weak and whose eyes are dim
But in whose heart love's fire burns bright?

We thank you Lord, for our dear old Mother,
And our poor gifts gladden her Jubilee.
God bless and crown her years of labour
And bless the years that are yet to be.

Early 1970s, Brisbane, Australia

12. The Reluctant MC

(Mother Teresa's Missionaries of Charity)

There was a certain MC who had a phobia,
Though she liked "Superiors" the office frightened her,
Oh not because she's humble, a lazy-bones is she,
Let others have the running and responsibility.

One day it is the current -- call the electricians in;
Another it's the parlour that makes her poor head spin.
Then suddenly a Sister has an accident,
Her toe or elbow's broken and she's got to get a splint.

You sit down of an evening to balance all the books
But someone comes to see you with catastrophic looks!
The dull headache of money, the stress of the bazaar,
The bank, the phone, the earthquake, Superior's pleasures
are.

"Sister, I've lost my needle! Sister, there's no more coal!
Sister, I've burnt the curry and all the soap's been stole!"
Dear me, the roof is leaking and blue-pars are out of stock!
The tube-well needs some nursing, the gate another lock!

Heavens, we'll all be martyrs, there's soda in the tea!
"I thought it was milk powder," Sister Cook smiles
innocently.
O hydra-head of business! O dragon-clasp of work!
If it's not the Corporation it's the letters you can't shirk!

O my tomorrow's Chapter -- what'll you talk about?
You've suddenly got lockjaw and cannot open your mouth!
They're awaiting your instructions, hands folded, eager-
eyed;
Your fluttering heart is dreading the last blow to your pride.

Of course there is the good side of being Superior,
To have your Sisters near you to help and soothe and cheer,
To see their good example with joy and gratitude,
To learn one's limitations with humble love imbued.

13. Scanned and Banned Except in Fun Land

This is a stupid title for a super original day,
Doing the most ordinary things in a truly extraordinary
way.
Noreen my friend and neighbour invested time and
planning
To make me take the put-off plunge like a bird on its first
migration,
The untried bus familiarised, the route untaken, taken.

At destination the King of kings disguised as bread is
waiting;
Mass at Saint Mary Mackillop Shrine, then Saint Paul's
next door for shopping.
We amble off … we're going to eat …
"The Cathedral Café?" I venture.
"Oh no, we can do better than that!
It's your birthday and I'm shouting."

Criss-crossing the masculine-feminine streets
we pad along the City.
Queen's Plaza yields up David Jones, its
Coffee and Chocolate location,
Cool, beautiful, soothing, pithy, and a lucky last table our
station.
Noreen orders emphatically:
"A cup of tea and sandwiched cheese."
For me, only "Filo with spinach, and a glass of

water if you please."
My messed up order comes in first, instead of spinach,
believe it, chicken!
But Noreen's bungle is a lot worse, salad and ham and
cheese only a smidgen!
Once the offenders are banished away Sherry, our little
waitress confesses,
"I am having a bad hair day!"

I glance at Noreen's cool cup of tea, the flash of a brew and
three-quarters milk,
(For me this is tea in the lowest degree!)
Thank you, dear friend, for the gift of a day, for all that you
are
And a meal that floundered -- a lunch that had a mind of its
own --
Which our fun and laughter only compounded!

Poems of Love and Loss

"In the eternity of morning freshness

In the eternity of evening rest

In the eternity of inaccessible light

I shall love my love forever."

Thank you, my unforgettable friend.

14. To My Mother

Eighty years have passed like yesterday
And the things that are, are not like the things that were;
The finger of time has touched each passing year
And scarce tomorrow comes but it's away.
Soon, very soon, I'll be with you again
Pouring out the pent up longing of many years
In unimagined joy, for all our tears
Will then be gone with unremembered pain.

Then I shall run to your welcoming embrace
And we'll forgive the wrongs we did each other --
You'll know I always loved you darling mother,
And ever longed to see at last your face.
Oh when its beauty shines upon my eyes
And our free souls in admiration gaze
Upon our glorious God in wondering praise
No other death shall rob our paradise.

My mother died on the 9th of March 1941 when I was 12. My father had already died eight years earlier when I was four. Now I am 96 and a half! I am sure they have parented me from their place in the Light. 22 July 2025

15. Beggars All

All that I had by Thee was given....
All that I lost by Thee was taken...
The giving seemed mutual between me and Thee.
I give? Nothing belonged to me.

And what Thou gavest I made my own
Forgetting it was but a loan.
Thus Lord, when Thou didst come to claim
Thine own, my heart was seared with pain.

Written for Bob Espe, American from Alaska who married our Joyce Stanley in India and took her to live on his huge estate. Her mother, my sister-in-law Birdeth married to my half-brother Nester Freese (both formerly widowed), used to share Joyce's letters with me -- ecstatic outpourings. In one of the last she had written: "I am too happy to live." The plane that was carrying her to hospital to have their second child crashed over Alaska and the wreckage was never found. With her was their small son Victor. It was 26 January 1950. She was 23 at the time and I, 21. The grief-stricken Bob was greatly moved by this poem and started writing to me, but when he said he was determined to return to India to marry one of her sisters or relatives, it seemed time to back off.

16. Wait For Me

Wait for me, my distant friend,
Delay a little yet your flight.
Wait and pray and watch with me.
All my longings are not yet done --
All my tears but half begun.
Wait for me, my distant friend,
God's gift to me for Earth's long night.

Will your leave me now so soon?
Will you start upon the road alone?
Will you go without fear across the wilds in the night?
Wait for me, my friend, it won't be long.
But oh, you do not heed, you hurry on.
Who will draw water for you on the way?
Who will crush the thorns from your path?
Who will spread a pillow for your tired head?
Ah my friend, wait for me…
If I could travel on your road
I would carry all your load.

But life moves slowly and time moves fast --
You have sped ahead of me.
Already my glimpse of you is now the last.
You have silently slipped away
Beneath the very eyes that saw you,
Was it yesterday?
Wait for me, my distant friend
Till we meet in Heaven, God's home at last.

Words

In memory of my American Jesuit friend, Father James Stuart Tong, S.J., 16 years my senior, one of the most loving and Christ-like priests I have ever known. He died in India in 1986, just before the release of my first book THE EYES ARE SUNLIGHT - A Journey Through Grief (Ave Maria Press, Notre Dame, Indiana, U.S.A.). There is a picture of him in my second book, LOVE IS MORE THAN ALL In the Here-and-Now and Ever-After (2023 InHouse Publishing, Brisbane; Amazon and Internet).

17. To Someone Dear

Why are you special? The reasons are so many
That I could not exhaust them though I wrote all day.
Not one has meaning. None, if any
Can sum you up, dear friend, in any way.
You are so clean for one thing, and so tidy
You smell so fresh and look so awfully good.
And then your temperament is temperamental,
You laugh and storm and banter when you would.
Another of your assets is your cooking,
Quite literally a meal at the drop of a hat,
As if it weren't enough that you're good-looking
And an actor, poet, artist and all that!
Many other things I like about you,
Your sense of fun, your triple-tier conceit,
Your weight of talent, your excelling patience,
Your self-discipline so hard to beat.
Each time I think that I have reached the limit
Of who you are, some new thing happens by
And then I realise it is not over,
I'll find new things in you until I die.
Even the lowly spider tastes your kindness,
You're sweet with animals and insects too.
That moth whose wings you dried, that butterfly,
Speak to my heart repeatedly of you.
And so, my friend, these and many others
Are the reasons why you're held so dear.
Not one has meaning, none could really tell you
Why to my heart and life you are so near.

18. Stranger, My Friend

Where are you going, stranger my friend?
Can I come too? Will you show me the way?
I know you so well, every line of your face
And yet you are strange like a far distant place.
Are you tired, my friend, of the weary day
And the long struggle, and the empty night?
Like a song that is stilled and an eye without light?
My heart cries out WHY? in Gethsemani.

Now I'm parched in the desert with nothing but sand,
My body stoned, my heart a knot,
And I am lonely in Earthland.
Go away stranger, don't come back,
You're too full of all that is close to me.
Will God forgive my need of you,
He who made us and gave us empathy?

Come no more, but still I'll wait
In case you do -- but stranger please,
Will you stop being you?
Oh, are your going -- going without me?
Not looking back, not saying goodbye?
Come back! Can't you hear me?
The road is so long, I'm afraid of the darkness --
Don't leave me alone.

No, don't come back, your lips aren't for me.
Go well, stay well, loved stranger,
And be happy.

Good Friday

Shirley Koers

19. Last Word

I take my pen to write of you
And cannot write a line.
I long to grasp the heart of you,
But I fail every time.
You are so wonderful, my friend,
You're all my hopes come true,
And if all earth were mine to choose,
Of all earth I'd choose you.

Exceeding rich my life has been
And many friends I've known,
But never one like you, my friend,
You stand apart, alone.
No Greek god could compare with you
In form, in wit, in sweetness,
Your sense of humour's wonderful,
You're full of all completeness.
You know just how to deal with me,
You know just when to tease!
You can be grave and full of fun,
And with you I'm at ease.
I'm glad dear friend I'm not your wife --
It would scare me through and through
To have a gold mine in my home
And "own" a man like you!

I'd love you till you died of it,
I'd worship at your shrine;
My heart could never bear the joy
Of having you for mine.

Words

In any case you are not free,
And calm has come from pain...
So goodbye my Platonic love
We will not meet again.

20. Inspired by "What Now My Love" (a song)

What now my love, this is our parting --
I could not think when you were near.
Now you are far and I am further --
What is left for me over here?

I ask my God just how much anguish
The heart can bear and still adore,
Between us the unfathomed ocean,
Beyond us is the tideless shore.

Unfathomed too are God's commandments:
Thou shalt DO, and Thou shalt NOT --
Alas my love, why do I love you
When life without you is my lot?

I waited years, sought down the ages
For love that would grow and never die,
And now, my love, now there is nothing,
Only my last goodbye.

21. Saint Valentine 1

Time stood still
The day, you brought me home
So accidentally,
And all my world was changed.
Time stood still
When you spoke poetry
And I longed to encompass
Your great sensitivity.

Time stands still --
Remembering you is pain
And ideals half forgotten
Now flare up again.
You are not free to love.
I cannot marry you.
The tears of things will pass
And life will too.

Were I some smouldering incense
I would cease to burn,
Were I some far-flung planet,
I would cease to turn.
Will you or I remember
Without knowing the reason why,
That to keep this special love
I said goodbye?

Alas the tears of things
Are mine and only mine.
Perhaps I will recover
In time… In time...

22. Saint Valentine 2

Stars spill from the Creator's hand
Like softly gleaming pearls of night
Meshed in their ancient mystery.
"Find me a star that shines for me,"
I prayed, searching their teeming eyes,
And looked at one that looked at me.
Wrapped, in a rainbow on a cloud
My wish sped through the Ever-Now
From world's first dark to world's last light,
Knocking, wayworn, from door to door.
Then came new music in my heart,
Within my arms a fresh bouquet,
All tenderly I took a flower
And laid it at the feet of day.

I sent it like a thought, a prayer,
But in my soul of darkest night
My sacrificial lamb I killed --
He was another's, never mine.
It was the piercing, turning sword.
It was the heart's love for my Lord.
Now in my arms a fresh bouquet
Upon my tomb of death from pain.

I loved again in after years,
A growing love beyond 'in love'.
Love is the heart's prerogative,
Love is its life, the self it gives.
Yet in the desert of the Void
I found all love is crucified,

And Love itself hangs on a Cross.
Live then forever, my only Love,
My living Life, Lord of my loss.

Shirley Koers

23. Thank You Jacobus (Jack)

Thank you for the things you do --
They mean so much these little things --
I could not measure all the joy
Your consideration brings.

Thank you for the things you are,
The constant, cheerful source within,
The sensitive and loving mind
That makes you special among men.

Thanks to you for being you
When times like ours are false and sick,
When faith burns low and hearts are cold
And men like you make this Earth tick.

I thank the Lord of light and love,
The King of hearts, who from his throne
Saw you and me and took the time
To lay your path across my own.

11 November 1975

24. A Sonnet For My Husband

"And in that hour and moment you were born"...
The world was changed, so was my destiny.
My life you entered unobtrusively
And brought the promise of a brighter dawn.
You are the rainbow riding on the storm,
The patient sweetness I could never be
With love unbounded reaching out to me
Till we are new in mutual love reborn.

You are my husband, time has made it so
And it shall be till time runs out of sand.
With all the heavens to roam where should I go,
For where you are is now my own homeland.
I'll have you as you are forever and aye,
Come life, come death, more precious every day.

6th July 1976, Napier, New Zealand. Written for his birthday the following day, the 7th. We were three months married. Two years later Jacobus would be dead on 6th October 1978 from smoker's lung cancer which became a brain tumor.

25. Only a dream

Only a dream it was
That woke me crying
Of someone who couldn't cope …
My husband dying.

I was across the Tasman
So unaware
That he had seven weeks to live
And I wasn't there.

O God of memory,
Lord of creation,
Remember when I come to you
I've had my purgation...

28 August 1978

26. G 0 D

My only prayer, one word -- GOD.
Cried from a heart bereft -- GOD. GOD.
God, can't I speak to you as others do?
Oh God... God ...

What does it mean to utter that word, GOD?
If only I knew.
GOD.
GOD -- perhaps it says I LOVE YOU.
Or perhaps I'M SORRY.
God. Is this your way with a mortal --
You transcendent --
making me feel the burden of you, GOD?

Written 7 December 1978, two months after my Jack (Jacobus) died.

Shirley Koers

27. On the Death of Jacobus (Jack)

Your precious earth is cold, my darling,
detached from me, withdrawn from time,
six weeks have passed like yesterday
since you were mine.

I looked at the Marriage Register
and saw our names, ink hardly dry,
but now you're on a different roll.
You've said goodbye.

I try to 'see' with eyes of Faith
and glimpse a fraction or your heaven,
but my cramped heart, too small for joy
is only broken.

That windmill scene on the calendar,
that framed Van Gogh, that book you've read --
wherever I look it's you I see --
can you be dead?

You'll never be warm to my touch again,
your tuneless tunes you'll sing no more,
your eyes will never light up to mine
as they did before.

I've waited, all my life, my darling,
I'm tired, so tired -- how long will it be
before the eternal arms of the Father
reach out to me?

17 November 1978

28. Wedding Anniversary

It's coming up,
Our third,
But you're not there.

I found it in a drawer,
The little card
Chosen so specially for that special day.

The sight of it --
Thick with memories --
Shrieks out your absence
Beyond recall.

You did not wait --
You could not.

I must learn patience too
As I learned tough love,
The hardest way.

14 February 1979

29. Pruning

I was content to be
A third-class rose bush full of mediocrity…
I found it hard to lose
One atom of my inselfness. If I could choose
I would have kept my dross
And gone my way unmindful of my loss.
My mediocre ways
I would have followed all my earthly days
And left unpurged my so selfish love,
Unmindful of lost graces from above.

And then You came along and cut
Into my being's core
And threw me from my safe secure
Spiritual rut,
And plucked me clean
Of all that was not You,
Though fresh and green,
The limbs that shrank in vain
From the relentless knife, crying out in pain.

Branch by branch You stripped me bare,
And took my Jack and left me all alone --
The only "family" I have ever known --
Now robbed of anchor I must find You there.
Yes Lord, I want to be
One of your miracles,
A perfect rose on a perfect tree.
Help me.
13 November 1978, five weeks after his death

Meditations in Verse

Love is the desire to live

that one may love more,

Love is the desire to love

that one may give more,

Love is the willingness to suffer

that love may be strengthened,

Love is the desire to die

that love may be fulfilled.

— Shirley Koers

30. The Three Circles (Inspired by a talk on the three stages of surrender)

Circle Number One
I reign here. This is MY throne.
In Ego territory I am all alone.
In this realm of inflated Pride
there's NO room for you and me inside.
Around me stark chaos, a life all awry,
sick with self-worship a dead king, I.

Circle Number Two
Lord, you have entered but I'm still boss.
Can't let you get too near -- stay down, Cross.
It's nice having you around but I like to be
All my own master, don't you see?

Circle Number Three
How did it happen, this great miracle?
You on my throne, Lord, high on a pinnacle?
Was it love melted me, broke my, heart in two?
Oh Lord, how wonderful to be kneeling to you!

30 November 1978

31. Kinds of Loving

I could pluck the rose --
enjoy its beauty, feast upon its scent,
take each petal ruthlessly apart
to feed the hunger of my searching heart
until my rose was dead, its perfume spent.

I could leave my rose upon the tree
and shut my eyes to its exquisite form
and never touch what was not meant for me --
deny my heart, leave it to blossom free,
to face the wind and rain and violent storm.

But oh, within the myriad stars of heaven
and countless worlds and living beings unknown,
can there be two kinds of loving only
on this Earth of ours, this planet home?
The rose so beautiful, the heart so warm,
they speak God's loveliness, they are his own.
Lord save me from the awful poverty
of a heart too crippled to love deep and free.

Then I will love the goodness that I meet
along life's way, making it so sweet,
unlocking the mind's interior door
to wonder, beauty, sweetness, more and more.
And give me, God of love, that tenderness
to foster, not destroy, life's loveliness.
To give all back to you from where it came,
made perfect, rich, and glorious, through your Name.

Then I will understand the things that are
the tears of things – and all the things that were.
Then I will see the purpose that you see
when you gave joy to one, pain to another, and hope to me.
All the unanswered riddles that are there,
all these are in your plan, they fit in place.
Lord, I shall know at last, and understand,
when I behold the glories of your Face.

32. Looking Ahead

A heap of clay, a stony block
Shapeless and dead.
From sculptor's hand and mallet stroke
Is born a head.
As chisel works perfection lives,
A form has grown...
Is God outdone, outfaced by pale
Genius in stone?

Then let the blows God deals in love
Fashion you through.
In his great mind he has conceived
Another you.

33. Pentecost Sunday

A beautiful view from a window
Overlooking the Bay
And ancient mountains wearing
New snow fallen today,
With lights and houses different
But stars the same I saw
On another stretch of heaven
Upon another shore.
Yet my inner view is wider,
The surrounds are radiances
Where all felt pain, all longing,
Turns to gentle cadences;
Where stark and harsh reality
Of earthly circumstance
And all its insecurity
Takes only this one stance:
The Lord has a Father's pity,
The Lord is Love itself,
His mercy is above his works,
His mercy is himself.

Within these secret pastures
The Spirit blows as he will
To teach, correct, encourage,
To restrain and to fulfil.
You cannot hold his sparkles,
His moment-to-moment blessings,
Unstorable like manna
They are not for your possessing.

Words

You cannot even remember
His so sweet and lovely words
That melt to the unreachable
Before you have dried your tears,
Before you can even capture
The unsharable to share
Because he has enough for all.
Holy Spirit is everywhere.

10 June 1984 - Napier, New Zealand

34. A Time for Growing

Because I hurt you,
you come nearer to me than those
whose hurt has never been because of me.

Because I caused your pain
I think more tenderly towards
the wounded heart of all mankind.

All the bright worlds
in all the turning galaxies
once saw Love broken on the Cross.

If I had not
put in those nails myself,
He never would have conquered me.

35. An Unexpected Prayer

Today I went a-walking… walking…
trying to pray my Rosary,
my head a melting pot of recent thoughts,
my heart divided between reveries.

Then suddenly I raised my eyes and there it was,
the brightest sky.
God's eyes are blue, I saw,
God's eyes are laughing blue,
and look! His hair is lily -white, and sun-baked gold,
and even raven-black when storms unfold.

This pond, these trees, these water birds,
have seen God from eternity,
and I have stumbled on him unawares
and oh so unexpectedly.

36. My Prayer, 0 Lord

When I am dying my comfort will be
That I said yes to you Lord in time and eternity,
Though I'm not a martyr bleeding or burning,
Nor can I be a saint with virtue unturning.
But what have I done for you in my time on Earth?
What can I offer you to validate my birth?
Still Lord, remember that I have loved
In my own little poor way, the best that I could.
Friends who enriched my life, you gave to me.
They made up for lack of kin, they were my theology.
Make me a new person, Lord, the prayer of faith my prayer,
Fill me with confidence in the knowledge you are there.
Please when your call comes in night or day,
Remember I am waiting. Don't turn away.
In kindness don't remember all the good I didn't do.
Just think, loved Redeemer, how much I wanted to love you.
Let me find less and less of me and more of you each day
And let the light of your glory not fail to come my way.
When I am dying, Lord, how happy I'll be
That things went your way, not mine, in time and eternity.

37. My God

Moses' God of Sinai is a world away from me,
The fire, lightning, thunder, inspired terror only.
The God I'd fall before upon my bended knee
Is he who came through Mary as a vulnerable baby.

The God-Man died for me on the hill of Calvary,
The crown set upon him was not of gold but of thorn;
Jesus bore it for my sin, his eyes stabbed, his flesh torn.
The God I know died for me in his humanity.

Loved to death we are, how could we throw out cold
His life and love given for us -- love so manifold?
Is Mary's tiny baby lying on cattle straw
To go unloved forever instead of more and more?

0 Father, Son and Spirit, immortal Trinity,
Our Lord and God forever, Love itself Divine Eternity.

38. Love Is...

Love is the highest good in life,
Love is a husband, love is a wife.
Love is also a furry kitten,
A songbird blending music unending,
And ramblers heavy with scent and bloom
And laughter of children playing at noon.

Love is also the friends who know
The thoughts within you that come and go,
Who tell each need, each one apart
And read the story of your heart,
To whom no secret is profane,
Who feel your every joy and pain.

Love is the standing back from love
And saying no while loving love.
Love is the tear that is not shed,
The touch withheld, the word unsaid.
Love is the beauty overflowing,
In the wide world past all our knowing.
Love is the rainbow floating high,
Love is the stars in the midnight sky,
The burning fire that does not grow cold
Or settle for things that are bought and sold.
Love is the prayer welling silently
For the lonely world and its tragedy.
Love is the baby that once lay small
On a heap of straw in a cattle stall.
Love is the Man through whom sin died,
Whom we have so often crucified.

Love is the question the whole world asks,
Love is the answer from first to last.
Love is the HOPE that never dies
In the face of injustice, deception and lies,
In the face of jealousy, lust and hate,
Love is the anguish of loving too late.
Oh Lord have mercy on the children of men
And heal our unloving. Amen. Amen.

39. Sonnet 1 -- The mysterious ways of love

Love's ways are various as the stars that shine
In different splendours, different harmonies;
Love begets love in strange realities
And goes beyond the reach of space and time.
To those who worship at its secret shrine,
Love promises the highest ecstasies
And holds within itself all mysteries
That touch the very heart of the divine.

Yet love, for all its greatness, came to me
Before I realised the spell was cast
And held my heart a captive, once so free,
And left me loved, and loving, full at last.
But earthly love was not for me I knew.
I turned away and bade my love adieu.

40. Sonnet 2 -- The mysterious ways of love

Love walked abroad within the universe,
Poured out his glories among every race,
Made beautiful the things most commonplace
And set man free from the eternal curse.
He spoke to man in language most diverse
And set him in his heart before his Face
And cured the follies selfishness made worse
That man committed as he sped through Space.

And this Love, incognito, speaks again:
"All that you have, I gave, all that you are...
The cost to Me was greater than your pain,
While you are whole, it's I who bear the scar."
Then come, dread Love, and make your home with me.
My earthly love I consecrate to thee.

41. All Things Pass

All things pass, fire turns cold,
Light burns out, youth grows old.
Flowers must wither, beauty fade at last,
Love too weakens that once held fast.

But you, Lord of Glory, are Friend who never fails,
Trust that never falters, love that still prevails.
You're the same forever, anchor of the weak,
Changeless and eternal, shepherd of your sheep.

You're the tender Saviour, I you wayward lamb,
Hold me on your bosom, just as I am.
Open to me the secret, unlock to me the door,
Let me grow less and less while you grow more and more.

42. Our Final Goal

My Lord, in long awaiting
I think of the precious day
When past, present and future
And time will melt away.
Over the waves of blue water,
Far where the oceans roll
Beyond desert sands of longing
Love itself is our final goal.

Oh Lord on that final journey
Will you be at my side
That we may explore together
Your universe vast and wide?
The stars in the secret heavens
Within the halls of Space,
Past the valley of silence
Will now be my dwelling place.

And all things now so real
Shall one day fade away
Like the wisp of a ghost body
That no desire can stay.
0 beautiful, beautiful story
Of all that is and shall be
When we have doffed our body
And live only, Lord, for Thee.

Now uncreated Beauty
Unveils his glorious Face --
From last back to first dreaming
Love is Love's long embrace.

Shirley Koers

43. Sing Beautiful Heavens

Sing, beautiful heavens,
Drop down dew,
Cover Earth with freshness,
Make all things new.

Tell once more the story
Of love transcending man,
Born in the Creator
Before time began.

Remember all your children
And remember me,
Someone who is all alone
The way you made me, me.

Beyond this vale of sadness
Your Beauty is revealed
And all life's hidden meaning
That is now concealed.

Sing, beautiful heavens,
Rain down from above,
Our Earth is parched and weary,
Thirsting for love.

44. Jerusalem

City of white and gold,
City of Solomon's glory,
Trysting of New and Old,
Prophets and Gospel story.

Bride of Messiah's love,
Child of Messiah's tears,
City of broken faith
And tragic, longing years.

City of ageless hope
Your King will come again,
And in the New Jerusalem
Eternally will reign.

45. Mary

Not one of all the thoughts that throng this brain
Take shape
To praise your heavenly beauty and your name;
Not one of all the fantasies I dream
Escape
Into the reality of you, my Queen.

For his earth-coming God prepared your soul
All pure --
Free from our shame and doom -- for your great role
In his Redemption's scheme, oh marvellous plan!
The Door
Through which he entered on the world of Man.
Mary, child of promise, hope shines anew;
The Fall
That blights the universe, stops short of you.
God deigns to glorify your lowliness
Of all
Nearest to him in perfect holiness.

46. Lullaby to the Holy Child

Let me be the little crib
To cradle you to sleep,
Let me be the shepherds lone
Watching their silent sheep.
Let me be the gleaming Star
That led the Magi home,
Let me be the frankincense
Of sweetness round your throne.

But more than all, O let me be,
While still no word is said,
That Maiden's heart that beat with love
Against your little head.

47. My Rosary

I love to pray my holy Beads
And to my Mother speak my needs.
To say a Rosary of red
And weep with Mary by her Dead.

And sometimes mysteries of white
To Maiden bowed in angel-light
I sing, repeating one by one
The Ave to God's chosen one.

Then golden Rosaries I say
To hail her on her Crowning day,
This simple girl with sinless eyes
Now glorious Queen of paradise.

A very early poem, perhaps going back to the 1960s.

48. The Fifth Joyful Mystery Of the Rosary

In the Fifth Joyful Mystery
it suddenly occurred to me
it was the Mother who'd been lost,
not just the Son,
and not for three days only
but for five centuries,
the Reformation separating
500 years of waiting
for the Mother and the Son
to be recognised as one.

The English Church reclaimed her,
their spiritual Mother named her,
but for the Protestant churches
Mother Mary faces
the separation from the Jesus
Christian churches of her Son.
There on Calvary and its Cross
Mother Mary faces the loss
of Jesus when he gave her
to John for everyone.

The Finding of the Child Jesus in the Temple after his three-day loss.
Scripture reference: Saint Luke's Gospel Chapter 2: verses 41-52
English Church: the Anglican Church
Protestant churches in the USA have been known to register up to 500
denominations in their directories as I found on one occasion, including a
Church of U.F.Os -- and why not? A good thing surely for those who believe in
them.

49. A Plea to the Mother of Jesus

Dearest Mother come for me
When my time on Earth is done,
Take today and take tomorrow,
Bring me safely to your Son.

I thank you for the countless blessings
Your great love has heaped on me
From the eternal arms of Jesus
In the glory of eternity.

How I need you, God's own Mother,
Night and day your powerful prayer,
Until I am safe in heaven
In your arms to thank you there.

50. Two People

If ever two were willed to meet
It was dear Tracey and her Louis,
What a tale of interventions
On the part of heaven's agents …
Happiness is their glorious witness,
Love that God gives radiating
A taste of heaven on their doormat
Witnessing love of God's creating.
As patron saints of ideal marriage
All differences unite above --
A visit from them is a visit
From Ambassadors of Love.

Shirley Koers
Brisbane Australia
Tuesday 12th August 2025
(the day they visited me on a three-day trip from Perth, Western Australia,
5000km away)

www.ingramcontent.com/pod-product-compliance
Lightning Source LLC
Chambersburg PA
CBHW050038040726

47599CB00015B/1741

not allowed unless with written permission from the publisher. All rights reserved.

The information provided herein is stated to be truthful and consistent, in that any liability, in terms of inattention or otherwise, by any usage or abuse of any policies, processes, or directions contained within is the solitary and utter responsibility of the recipient reader. Under no circumstances will any legal responsibility or blame be held against the publisher for any reparation, damages, or monetary loss due to the information herein, either directly or indirectly.

Respective authors own all copyrights not held by the publisher.

The information herein is offered for informational purposes solely, and is universal as so. The presentation of the information is without contract or any type of guarantee assurance.

The trademarks that are used are without any consent, and the publication of the trademark is without permission or backing by the trademark owner. All trademarks and brands within this book are for clarifying purposes only and are the owned by the owners themselves, not affiliated with this document.

Chapter 1. The Importance of Focus & Concentration

With focus and concentration you're going to find more peace and success in your life. You need to stay focused to achieve goals, and if you lack focus and concentration for any reason, then you're going to have issues succeeding and finding happiness. You're going to feel much more peaceful if you have focus, and that is because you aren't' wasting your time on anything that you don't want to do for longer than you have to. Everyone has been that kid once or twice where they dragged out a homework assignment for at least twice as long as it would have taken if they had decided to buckle down and focus. However, it's not always as easy as just buckling down for some people.

Some people have an actual issue with focus and improving their concentration, and that includes both adults and children with either ADD or ADHD. During these times, focus and concentration can become harder than it already is, and it's not easy feat to accomplish in the first place. In this book, you'll learn various ways to improve your focus and concentrations o you can find peace and success in your own life.

Concentration and Creativity:

Some people are under the delusion that focus and concentration can actually suppress creativity, but this is actually a myth. If you are focused and concentrating on what you are doing, then you are more likely to create something beautiful, unique, and useful. Many creative types know that focus is important, and it helps them to promote their skills and apply it in a way that will lead to success instead of deter them from it. It doesn't matter if you're going to be an artist or a doctor because focus and concentration is needed no matter what field you plan to study and pursue for the rest of your life.

If you're still wondering how focus can help you even with your creativity, then you need to think about it for a moment. Every writer needs to focus on what they're doing. It doesn't matter if they're writing for a journal or if they're writing for a blog. They have to be able to focus and concentrate on what they're doing if they want to do it right, effectively, and efficiently. They also need to be able to increase their concentration on their business as a whole. Even if you're just creating a product, from an app to a new form of energy, it doesn't matter because focus and concentration are going to be necessary for this as well. It'll cut the time you work in half, and it'll help you achieve every goal that you set in front of you.

Goal setting is great, but if you don't have the concentration to continuously push forward to achieve these goals, then it will only blow up in your face. So do yourself a favor, and work on keeping a steady focus and concentration on anything you set your mind to. You'll be happier and more successful. It can help anyone, and it's in the reach for everyone. There's no reason to stress over it.

Don't Get Stressed:

You don't need to be stressed out just because you can't focus. You'll actually find that by increasing your concentration and focus you're going to decrease the stress that you're feeling. It'll allow you to narrow in on what you're doing, blocking out the distractions that keep you from being where you want to be in life. This will directly lead to you being a happier and more peaceful person. Someone who feels unfulfilled, which will happen if you are failing at achieving your goals due to a lack of concentration, will be unhappier than a person who feels that they can reach for the stars and actually achieve.

There's no reason to feel overwhelmed. Even if it isn't easy for you to focus now, it'll become easier with the methods that this book describes. You can start with something as simple as meditation, but if you're really having issues, you can go all the way to herbal remedies that will help to increase your concentration naturally. Don't turn to synthetic drugs with chemicals that could have harsh side effects on your mental and emotional state as well as your body. These natural alternatives will work, and they'll especially work in the long run. Anyone and everyone can help to increase their focus and concentration. For some people, these methods will work immediately, but for other's it may take a little more effort.

It doesn't matter which category you fall into because it's still possible. Just keep trying, and there is something for everyone. Focus on moving forward, and that's your first step to increasing your concentration. Your focus will sharpen, and with it so will your determination to succeed. Success comes naturally afterwards.

Chapter 2. How Meditation Helps You to Improve

Meditation is one of the easiest and natural ways to improve your concentration and focus, but you'll find it doesn't work immediately. It takes time, and you have to continue to pursue meditation at least once daily. If you're trying to increase your concentration and see results faster, then you're going to want to work meditation into your daily schedule at least twice a day, but doing it once a day will help as well. Most people find that meditation works best if it's done in the morning, helping you to prepare for the day to come.

Why It Helps:

Meditation isn't what most people think it is. Most people think that meditation is about clearing your mind, but this isn't what meditation is meant to be. Meditation is meant to be focusing on one thing and only one thing. If you can meditate properly, you can hold your focus on a single item for prolonged periods of time. It doesn't matter if it's for five minutes or an hour. The more you meditate, the easier it becomes to do so for longer periods of time, and this is because your concentration and ability to focus is increasing over time. It's just a natural side effect of meditation.

Breathing meditation is actually one of the easiest ways to start, and that's because you're concentrating on a natural process that will occur anyways. This will allow you to focus on a sensation, which helps your mind to zoom in because it's zooming in on something that you can actually sense instead of a single idea or thought.

Anyone Can Accomplish It:

Don't be discouraged because it takes time that needs devoted to it. It isn't as quick as an herbal remedy, but it's still a viable option for almost anyone. Meditation doesn't require a large chunk of time. You can meditate for just five minutes a day or more if you have the time, but that five minutes will be enough to help you increase your concentration and focus. You don't have to be in nature, but many people find that meditating in their backyard where they're in a natural environment works best.

You can even meditate on the bus to work or while you're waiting on your coffee. It's all about centering your focus and using it like you would a mental muscle so that it builds up. The reason people think that a calmer environment works better, especially if you're just starting, is because a calm environment already minimizes the distractions that you are experiencing. It will help you to grasp the meditation process a little easier and expand your focus and concentration a little quicker.

A Meditation Walk Through:

You already know that meditation can actually help you accomplish your goal, but that doesn't mean you know where to start. This is one simple mediation that you can start, but there are many forms of meditation out there, including mindfulness meditation which many people will turn into a lifestyle. Meditation is going to also alleviate your mood and reduce any stress that you may be feeling. In extension, this will eliminate emotional and mental distractions while you're trying to work for the day.

This is a breathing meditation exercise, and you are going to want to start in comfortable clothes that won't distract you as well as starting in a comfortable position. If you aren't worried about falling asleep, many people will lay down to mediate. Other people find that sitting up is better, but make sure that you aren't uncomfortable in the position that you choose. Close your eyes so that you can block out visual distractions why you try to concentrate.

Start by taking one deep breath. In and out, and then when you exhale, let your breathing level back to normal. Focus on what it feels like to breath. Don't entertain any thoughts that aren't directly related to your breathing, as these thoughts will make you lose your focus. Let all thoughts fade, and don't listen to them. Listen to the sound that you make when you breathe and how your body responds.

Remember that you shouldn't move. You shouldn't allow yourself to get fidgety, as that is another sign that you're losing your concentration on what you're doing. You need to sit still, which is a foreign practice for many people. You need to control your physical body. It only moves if you allow it, so concentrate. When you're sitting comfortable, this becomes a little easier. You shouldn't succumb to movement unless you're actually in pain.

Next, you are going to want to concentrate on a mantra that is related to focus and concentration. You're going to want to shift your concentration to your mantra, which should be prepared beforehand if you plan to customize it. You should know exactly what you're going to say, and that's why you can recall it and bring it to the forefront of your mind.

"I am able to focus. I am able to concentrate. I can reach success." This is the mantra that many people suggest, as it is an affirmation of the positive thoughts that you should already be thinking, and it'll help you to directly relate what you are doing with your lack of concentration or focus in your everyday life. Continue to repeat the mantra every time you breathe out. With every breath, you should be repeating your mantra. You shouldn't mess up if you're holding your focus.

Having a mantra is another way to clear your thoughts. If you are concentrating on those words, then your mind is preoccupied, keeping you from actually thinking about anything else. This is yet another way it helps you to sharpen your concentration. After a few minutes, you can stop, going back to concentrating on the silence and your breathing. Then, you can open your eyes when you feel comfortable doing so. Do this at least once daily if you want to have success in increasing your concentration. After meditation, most people feel a little more focused and determined to get through whatever the day throws at them.

Kids Can Use It:

It doesn't matter what age you are. You'll find that meditation can help you, and it helps to alleviate your mood as well. Just keep in mind that younger children are going to have a harder time mediating despite being able to accomplish. If you are trying to teach your child to mediate, you are going to need to start slow, and it is recommended that you start in five minute intervals and increase it from there. Meditation will increase their focus, and it'll help them to concentrate on their schoolwork, homework, and even help their memory as a side effect of their focus and concentration being sharper. This will help to set them up for success, but it has benefits no matter how old you are as well.

Chapter 3. Modifying Your Behavior to Modify Your Focus & Concentration

There are many habits that you can incorporate into your daily routine to help increase your focus and concentration as well, and these habits will help you in the long term as well as the short term. With many of these habits, you'll notice some immediate effects, and before long they'll become natural as well. When habits become second nature, your focus and concentration will increase while you do them and even when you forget to do them, but your memory will also start to increase as your focus does.

This will help you to remember things as well. For example, going grocery shopping without focus can mean that you spend more money and waste more time, and you may even have to go multiple times. However, if you had focus when you were grocery shopping, you would have been able to spend only what you needed and wanted, went once, and gotten it done quicker.

Habit #1 Start Fresh

Try to complete everything you need to in one day, and if it is a goal that you can't actually complete in one day, break it up into smaller goals that you can. Everything should be on a day to day basis if you want to be able to concentrate on the here and now and focus on each task as it is on hand. This is why writing it down will help, but you can't allow yourself to become overwhelmed. When you feel that you're becoming overwhelmed, make sure that you remember that each day is a fresh start. Each day is new, and you have the ability to turn it into a positive experience. So, think about your first task and try not to think about the task that is going to come afterwards. Ignore what has to be done next. Clear your mind, just like you did with meditation so that the one item you're focusing on is prominent in your mind.

Habit #2 Write It Down

It may seem simple, but so many people who suffer from focus related issues, such as ADD and ADHD do not write things down. Writing what you need to do down is extremely important to help you focus. Everyone loses focus occasionally, but if you're having focus issues, you are going to have a harder time refocusing than other people. When you lose your train of thought, it may become frustrating if you have no help refocusing. However, if you have what you need to do written down. Then when you need to refocus, you only have to look at the list. This will also help to cut down the time you spend on something in half. You won't have to spend time trying to think of how to go about something or figuring out what you were supposed to do when you've lost the thought. It'll also help you to look at everything in a manner that allows you to take each step individually.

Habit #3 Set a Schedule

Setting a schedule is the first part of keeping to a schedule. If you know you're on a time limit, then you're more likely to try to increase your focus just so that you don't fall behind. This is why children will do schoolwork better than they do homework. With school they have that one period of time to get their work done because they can't do it at home. However, if they have homework they have a much longer period of time and much less accountability. A schedule that is tighter gives you that accountability, and it'll urge you to keep moving forward, which is impossible without the proper concentration and focus.

It'll help you to tackle everything that you've written for that day. this doesn't mean that you have to have an hour to hour schedule, but you should have a select period of time set aside for tasks that need done that day. For example, you may set the time for doing dishes at three, but you shouldn't pretend that you have all day to do the dishes. Set the time to three to four, and then you know you need to concentrate on getting that task done before the hour is up so you aren't behind.

Habit #4 Make a Distraction

It may seem counterproductive, but realize that something is going to distract you. You are capable of multi-tasking, and when you create your own distraction, that is your way of multi-tasking. Multi-tasking will also make you create a focused environment, and that is why the distraction that you make is technically a concentrated distraction. For example, when you're sitting there trying to do homework, you may want to put music on in the background.

That music serves as your distraction, but it also serves to block out any and all background noise, canceling out the many more distractions that you'd be experiencing without it. Of course, a concentrated distraction doesn't have to just be something you listen to, but that does work best for many people. This distraction can also be doodling with your pencil or tapping your foot. Physical actions are also great distractions because it brings your focus back to a sensation, which is why breathing meditation helps to focus you as well.

Habit #5 Create Specific Mantras

You can use a mantra outside of a meditation session as well, and that will help you to increase your focus. However, when you're trying to complete a task at hand, you aren't going to want to have a mantra that is an affirmation. You are going to want a mantra that is created specifically for what you are doing. A single word mantra often works best if you're using a mantra to increase focus during activities. When you concentrate on that one word, then you are brought back to what you're doing, and it'll help you to block out anything else that threatens to distract you. For example, when you're trying to do dishes, if you keep repeating the word dishes in your head, you won't ever forget what you're doing. You'll be concentrating on repeating that word as well as the action that is behind the word.

Stack Them Up:

Habit stacking is a common way to reach success. It's all about taking small habits and stacking them together to make a larger life change. When you apply one of the above habits to your daily routine, then you're already helping to reach your goal. However, when you stack all five habits into your daily routine, then you're going to reach that goal much faster. It'll focus your energy and your mind. It'll help you to even block out anything that may be harmful to reaching that goal.

Chapter 4. Foods to Eat to Help Improve Over the Long Term

The nutrients that you take in are also known to affect your concentration, and it'll help you to even fight off symptoms of ADD and ADHD. However, to gain this benefit you need to make sure that you're concentrating on eating the right foods and getting the right nutrients to help you concentrate more. Try to eat at least some of these foods each and every day, and then you'll find that it works more in the long term. It doesn't provide short term results, but long term results are going to what causes you to live a more focused and peaceful life.

Blueberries:

Almost everyone loves fruit, and it's easy to eat fruit every single day. Blueberries are going to help you to improve, and that's because they're antioxidant rich. It'll help to boost your memory as well, which will keep you focused long term. Blueberries are commonly added into your breakfast, but they can also be used as a snack. It doesn't matter if you're eating the blueberries fresh or dried, but they shouldn't be baked. Just make sure that you eat blueberries because they'll activate brain protecting enzymes, which will help as you reach old age as well. This way your focus is less likely to diminish with age as well.

Avocado:

Avocado is yet another thing that you can add, and it doesn't matter if it's cooked. You'll find that it'll help you either way, and that's because it has healthy fats that will help to increase your brain function. This will naturally increase your concentration with little effort. Of course, it always helps when you add healthy habits as well. It will also help with nutrient absorption, which will help the other foods to help a little more as well, making it a wonderful food to add to your normal routine.

Green Tea:

Most people know that caffeine can help you focus, but too much isn't good. Too much caffeine can actually make you too jittery to focus. Green tea has some caffeine, but it's that perfect balance for most people, especially those with ADD or ADHD. It'll even help you feel sated if you're hungry, and it'll help you to feel fuller longer when you're drinking it hot especially. The only calories that green tea has comes from the sweeteners that you have in you. If you're having a hard time with concentration, it is not recommended to add sugar, but you can use honey as a natural sweetener for your green tea.

Dark Chocolate:

Sadly, it's not any chocolate that will help you with focus, but if you love dark chocolate then you're in luck when you try to increase your concentration. Dark chocolate is known to help because it has a natural stimulant. Stimulants are known to keep you awake and help you to focus on the task at hand. You don't need a lot of dark chocolate, and that means often you won't even need to eat an entire bar. Sometimes, a few squares, depending on the size, is often enough. It also helps to decrease any sugar cravings that you may be having, which will often distract you while you're trying to do something.

Water:

Yes, it's that simple to increase your focus. If you're dehydrated, then you're not focusing well, and it isn't just because you're distracted because of the thirst. When you're not getting enough water in your diet, then your brain doesn't have the electrolytes it needs to function properly. This will make you more likely to lose your concentration even on simple tasks. Make sure that you are drinking water throughout the day to have better overall concentration. Everything that your body does will depend on water, and drinking more will keep you healthier and happier as well.

Flaxseed:

Not everyone wants to munch on flaxseed, but you can add it into your meals that you cook or even into a smoothie recipe. If you're a smoothie lover, it'll help to thicken your smoothie and make it more satisfying while still providing you a concentration boost. You'll find that they have B-vitamins, magnesium, fiber, and even omega-3 fatty acids, which all have been proven to help increase your concentration. It's considered a superfood for many of the reasons listed above, and it is known to help keep you full. This will help keep hunger from distracting you as much as well.

Fatty Fish:

The main example is salmon, and it's a great food to eat for a variety of reasons, but it's often considered a brain food for its focus boosting abilities. This is because it'll help you to get the omega-3 fatty acids that you need to increase your brain function and focus throughout the day. Fish can be used for just about any meal of the day, and some people actually eat fish and rice for breakfast, and it's very healthy for you. Just work fatty fish into your diet when you can if you're having focus issues. It can even help with depression, fatigue, and even mood swings. All of which can decrease your focus if you're suffering from them. Kipper, trout, mackerel, herring, and sardines are other fatty fish that can help.

Kale:

Kale is just one of the many leafy greens that can help you with your focus and concentration issues. Almost every leafy green has what you need for your problem, and they're easy to add into your diet and daily regime. If you don't want to cook with these foods, just blend them into a fruit smoothie, and other than the color you'll most likely not even realize that they're there. They're antioxidant rich, just like blueberries, and they contain the B-vitamins that your brain needs to keep your concentration sharp.

Nuts:

Nuts are also going to help you to improve, and it can be as simple as picking up a pack of peanuts. They're easy to add in as a snack, and often you'll find many nuts prepackaged so that they're easy to take with you, making it even simpler. Protein is needed for your brain to function properly, and if your brain is falling behind, then you're focus is already ruined for the entire day. It'll also keep you full so hunger won't be as big of an issue. You'll also find that it has vitamin B3 which is a B-vitamin that is needed for concentration.

Try One or More:

It is best that you eat these focus increasing foods as much as you can, but as a rule of thumb you should try to eat one or more every single day. If you can find a way to combine them that allows you to eat more than one a day, then you're already ahead of schedule, and it'll help you to increase your focus quicker. It'll even have the added benefit of helping to improve your health. Just like habit stacking, using more than one is best.

Chapter 5. Natural Vitamins & Supplements to Try Out

If you think that taking a pill is still easier, then that doesn't mean that you have to go the unnatural route. There are many vitamins and supplements out there that will help you with your issue, even if you have something as small as a bad attention span or if you really suffer from ADD or ADHD as an adult or as a child. The supplements and vitamins below can often be found at a natural food store, but many supermarkets will carry them as well. Just remember that you should talk to your doctor before adding any of these vitamins and supplements to your daily regime, especially if you are already taking over the counter medication or prescription drugs.

Cod Liver Oil:

You may find it in its oil form, but it's not recommended to take it that way due to the horrible taste. Of course, you can usually find a gel pill version of it, which will allow you to take it without the horrible taste. It has an added benefit of being great for the immune system, but it'll help to focus you as well. It's been shown to help with ADHD symptoms, even in children. You can even take it while you're pregnant, as it'll help your baby's brain as well. This is a type of fish oil, and it has many healthy omega-3 fatty acids in it. It's best to take with food to keep from belching. It'll get rid of any aftertaste faster as well.

Zinc:

Zinc is known for calming people, but that's one of the reasons it's also recommended that you take it at night. It'll help detox and boost your immune system. It's great for attention disorders because of its calming effect. If you're calmer, then you're more likely to be able to concentrate when you need to because your mind isn't bouncing form one thing to the other. You shouldn't take it at the same time you take magnesium or calcium if you're taking those supplements, though. This is because it'll disrupt the way your body absorbs those two supplements. Try to always take zinc with food, or you're likely to feel very nauseous.

B-12:

Almost everyone knows that B-12 is helpful, and it's a great way to boost your energy. However, it can also boost your concentration. It's been recommended by many doctors for children who are suffering from ADD or ADHD. It'll help to ensure that your brain is function properly, as it won't if you have a B-12 deficiency. Not having enough B-12 doesn't just effect your focus, but it can actually cause disorientation and memory loss as well. You can get B-12 from cheese, eggs, and milk, but it's not usually enough if you already have a hard time focusing.

Vitamin C:

Focus is a part of your cognitive function, which can be increased through vitamin C. It'll affect your attention, and it has a lot of antioxidants. A great source of vitamin C is oranges, but there are many vegetables that you can use as well. If you feel that you aren't getting enough vitamin C in your diet, talk to your doctor about it or take a natural vitamin C supplement. It'll protect your brain against damaging free radicals which cause cell damage. If you want to get vitamin C in a more natural way try broccoli, bell peppers, or even spinach.

Niacin:

Just be aware that niacin can cause flushing or heat flashes, and if you're experiencing these then you need to talk to your doctor immediately. However, niacin is also a great supplement to add in if you're having issues focusing throughout the day. Your brain actually needs the niacin because it has vitamin B-3 in it. Without niacin, bad concentration will follow, and you may even experience common confusion and memory loss. It can all be avoided. You may not be getting enough niacin in your diet, even though it comes from whole grains, fish, potatoes and poultry, and a supplement is usually the answer.

B-6:

By now you already know that B-vitamins are extremely important to brain function and relate directly to concentration, and that includes vitamin B-6. You can use it on your own, or you can get a mixture like a complex, which is also sold in various natural health and food stores, as well as most supermarkets. It'll usually be paired with vitamins that help with absorption as well as assimilation. It's taken best when combined with magnesium, which is also recommended to increase concentration, and you can take both with a meal if you really want to get the most out of it. Keep in mind that if you have ADHD, you may already have a vitamin B-6 deficiency, as most people with ADHD do. You can always ask your doctor to check, and decide to add a B-6 supplement to your daily regime from there.

Magnesium:

Magnesium is a great supplement to take if you're still having issues, and it can be paired with almost any other supplement, making it even better to use. Magnesium doesn't affect focus directly, but it will help to relax you, and it will help to relieve tension that could be distracting you. It is known to help if you're distracted over most stressful situations, and it works with most B-vitamins, which are helpful directly with concentration issues. Just remember to never take too much, as it can cause diarrhea if you do. Just remember not to take it within two hours of taking zinc, as you won't absorb it as well as you should if you do. Magnesium increases the absorption of most B-vitamins.

Vinpocetine:

This isn't a supplement that you'll hear often, but it's great for your brain overall. It'll help your focus, your memory, your mental well-being and even your reaction time. It helps you to complete task as little quicker, and it does this by helping to increase the blood flow to your brain, which will in turn help to enhance its use of oxygen. It'll keep your brain from being damaged by free radicals.

Gingko Biloba:

Gingko biloba, often shortened to Gingko, is a great way to increase your concentration and help a lot of brain related issues. It can help with confusion, anxiety, depression, headaches, fatigue, and even forgetfulness. You can take it in its supplement form, but other people will add the powder into their teas, juices, or even their smoothies.

A Multi-Vitamin Helps Too:

Of course, if you don't have any of these and have no way of getting them anytime soon, you can start with a multi-vitamin which is going to help as well. This is really important if you are suffering from ADD or ADHD and that is causing your concentration and focus problems, and that is because if you suffer from these conditions then you are more likely to have vitamin deficiencies that are contributing to it or causing it directly. A multi-vitamin on a daily basis is one of the first steps to take in order to help to control the problem.

Chapter 6. Why Your Sleep Schedule is Important & Herbs to Help

Sleep affects the way that your brain functions, and if you are lacking sleep then you're likely working with only half the brain power that you should be working with. This will automatically decreases your focus and your concentration. Having a hard time sleeping in the first place isn't an excuse for letting it continue. There are many ways to help you increase your sleep, and there are many ways to increase your quality of sleep as well. For example, if you're practicing meditation, then you already have a tool that will help you to sleep more. Mediation will help you to get rid of stress and relax your body, which promotes healthier sleep. Meditation before bed is recommended if you want to achieve better sleep to help you with your concentration issues.

What Lack of Sleep Causes:

If you truly want to know why getting enough sleep will help you to increase your focus throughout the day, you need to understand how lack of sleep can affect your body and brain function. The bottom line is that it will affect your central nervous system, which is vital to proper concentration and focus. Without your central nervous system working properly, it'll be nearly impossible to achieve proper focus. The brain rests the neurons and it'll form new pathways so that you can get up in the morning, but only if you are getting the sleep that you need. It's especially important in children and young adults, but it's important to anyone no matter the age. It'll also help to produce the proteins that you need, as you need these proteins to repair cell damage.

Your brain is exhausted if you aren't getting enough sleep, and this is going to keep you distracted and unable to focus. It won't be able to perform at the level that it should, and it'll keep you from focusing on anything new especially. This is why a lack of sleep will directly impact your ability to learn new things and accomplish your goals that you've set in front of you. It even affects your memory, and memory is an important part of focusing on what you should do.

Feeling Sleepy is Detrimental:

Just the feeling of being sleepy is sure to mess you up when you're trying to concentrate and get something done. Think about all of the times that you've showed up to school or work tired. You probably weren't nearly as productive as you usually would be, and that's because the feeling of sleepiness is a distraction that you just don't need if you're trying to be productive. It'll also affect your decision making, so you're less likely to stick to any schedule that you've made, and it'll affect your memory. You may not even remember everything that you should be doing, which also stifle your creativity. If you are overly sleepy, you're going to be affected emotionally. Negative emotions are also a distraction. Turmoil emotions in general will keep you from accomplishing everything that you want to and impair your cognitive function.

Natural Solutions:

There are natural solutions to help you with sleep, and the first one is that you should try to get yourself on a natural sleep schedule. You're going to get more rest if your body is used to sleeping at a certain time. However, if it's not then it doesn't know when it should be sleeping and when you need it to stay awake. Start by trying to set a bedtime. If you already have one but it's late in the night, try to go to sleep thirty minutes earlier and wake up thirty minutes earlier. This will help many people increase their focus throughout the day. Of course, it sometimes isn't enough if you're having a hard time falling asleep in the first place. There are natural solutions for that as well.

Try out chamomile. It's a relaxing herb that is often found in the form of tea, and it's easy to drink right before bed. It's also known to help lower your stress and anxiety, helping to increase the quality of sleep that you'll be getting as well. If you're having a hard time relaxing your muscles, then you need to try chamomile. You can make it yourself from chamomile flowers, but you could always buy a premade tea as well, and many people find that it's much easier to do so. Remember that if you're trying to go to sleep you should never add sugar to a tea that's meant to help. Instead, if you want to sweeten it, try adding honey.

A hot bath is also known to help you to sleep, and there's actually a reason behind it. When you take a hot bath, you're going to raise your body temperature slightly, and that will make your temperature drop when you get out. This tells your brain that it's preparing for sleep, and if you take a warm bath before bed you can trick your brain into thinking your body was already preparing to send a signal to help you sleep.

Remember to cut the caffeine, even in your food, if you are having an issue with sleeping. This is because caffeine is a stimulant, and you shouldn't have it a good four hours before bed. So skip the dark chocolate for a dessert if you're looking to sleep anytime soon afterwards. You're also going to want to skip any coffee, energy drinks, or natural forms of caffeine so that you're prepared to go to bed and there's nothing in your body that's trying to keep you up.

Waking Refreshed:

When you wake refreshed, your concentration is already there and you'll be able to focus throughout the day. your body has been able to repair damage, allow you to wake up with a new day in mind, and you'll be able to look right over at the schedule that you've made to make sure you skip to the first thing that you should be focusing on. if you have to use caffeine, then do so, but if you want to get your focus up and running properly before you get too far into your day in a more natural manner, then try meditation first thing in the morning. Just make sure that you sit up so that you don't fall right back asleep.

Chapter 7. Natural Herbs That'll Do the Trick

There are many herbs that will help to increase your focus as well, and taking them in something as simple as a tea or a capsule is a great way to make sure that you are controlling your focus and taking your concentration issue into your own hands in a natural manner. No matter how you take them, these herbs need to be taken internally to do any good, and they've been proven to help even if you're suffering from ADD or ADHD.

Lemon Balm:

It belongs to the mint family, and that's the main reason that it's put into tea. The scent is known to help as well, but it is known to improve overall mental performance, and it increases your attention span over time as well as doing so short term. You'll find that it will also help the memory power in children, which is why it's put into many ADHD formulas. It will relieve most nervousness and anxiety, and it helps to increase your patience as well, which will allow you to focus on a particular activity for longer periods of time. It will help to relieve any restlessness that you're feeling right away.

Ginseng:

Natural stimulants are already known to help with ADHD, ADD, and general focus issues. That's why it is great when you use it as an herb to help you increase your concentration. It'll help you to improve your memory as well. It will regulate the way that your body releases energy, which helps to reduce hyperactivity and provide you energy throughout the day instead of in manic boosts. It will also help to decrease any impulsive behaviors that could be taking away from your focus.

Passionflower:

Passionflower may be a flower, but it's also an herb that will help you with your concentration problems. Just don't take too much of it, as it is known as a sedative. If you relax your body, then you're also going to relax your mind, decreasing any anxiety that could be causing you to become too easily distracted. The calming affect will also help to relieve any muscle spasms that you may be experiencing. It can help with insomnia as well, so take it before bed to help promote sleep. Once again, you can actually find it in both its capsule form, tincture form, as well as a tea form.

Brahmi:

This herb is going to help rejuvenate your brain as well as your nervous system, and it'll help both sides of your brain to work better together, increasing your overall mental function. It's known to help improve how fast you take in new information, and it'll help with your concentration by increasing your attention span, relieving anxiety, improving your immune system and even helping you to withstand more emotional distress. It can even help with insomnia, making it an herb that comes highly recommended if you're fighting any focus issues.

Vacha:

This is an herb that literally translates into the world speech, and it's great of the brain. It's known to promote better concentration right away, and it even has long term effects. It'll also help with clarity, and it treats any mental sluggishness that you may be feeling as well as any depression. You'll find that it'll detoxify your brain tissue, which will help to increase your memory and focus.

Rosemary:

Rosemary is also going to help to increase your concentration levels, and one of the best parts is that it's usually found right in your kitchen cabinet. It's okay to use both dried and fresh rosemary, so don't go out of your way to get one or the other. Either will do the trick, and that's because it's known for memory improvement. There's a direct correlation between a good memory and a good attention span because you're less likely to be distracted if you aren't having issues remembering what you're doing and what you want to accomplish.

It even has the added benefit of helping muscle pain, so if you're experiencing any muscle pain, it won't be as severe meaning it won't be as distracting. You don't even have to take it internally, as it can be used in aromatherapy to boost concentration levels as well. Rosemary oil can burn to help you focus and increase your attention span.

Basil:

Basil can also be found in your kitchen cabinet, and basil is easy to use to help to increase your attention span. It'll help to give you a break from mental fatigue, but it'll also help to increase your attention span directly. It doesn't matter if you consume or smell it, as it is able to be used in aromatherapy as well, but actually consuming it will help you to get more benefits from it. It will also help with depression and migraines, which will distract you from reaching your goals. You can use it in as an essential oil, and many people will rub it on their temples, helping them to focus right away. It works bet if you're using it on a regular basis, but it will help if you use it occasionally. It just won't help as much as it could.

Increasing Mental Fortitude:

If you want to increase your mental fortitude and attention span as a whole, you're going to want to use these herbs on a regular basis. It doesn't matter if you're using them in their dried, fresh, or essential oil form, but just use them. You can use most all of these herbs together, and in the herbal remedies below

you'll find a way to use most of them on a
regular basis without too much hassle.

Other Herbs Can Also Help:

You'll find that there are other herbs that will
help you to improve your attention span
indirectly as well. For example, if you are too
stressed out, then you aren't going to be able to
focus on you want to focus on. If you take herbs
that are going to help you to relieve your stress,
then you're starting to contribute to increasing
your attention span just like you would if you
took an herb that contributed directly.

Of course, if you're already taking chamomile,
making sure that you're getting enough sleep,
meditating, and dealing with any vitamin
deficiencies that you may be experiencing, then
these are already helping to lower your stress
and anxiety levels, which will help to stave off

depression. It all works together, and that's why making a regime that has you take various supplements, foods, and remedies will do the most good for your attention span. Good habits and what you consume will balance out into making sure that your attention span stays where it should be.

Chapter 8. Teas & Drinks That Will Naturally Help You

You have already learned many different herbs and supplements that are going to help you with your attention span. Despite knowing the herbs, you may not know how to use them, and there are still many other herbs that contribute to a better attention span and level of focus as well. This chapter is dedicated to a few recipes that you can use every day to increase your concentration and brain function as a whole. They have other benefits that come along with the remedy as well.

Drink #1 A Blast of Focus

If you're looking for something cold, then you're going to find that this smoothie is a great way to boost your focus almost immediately. Many people find that it's a great way to start your day as well.

Ingredients:

1. 1/3 Cup Fresh Blueberries
2. ¼ Cup Whole Milk
3. ¼ Cup Ice
4. ¼ Cup Strawberries
5. 1 Teaspoon Flaxseed
6. 2 Teaspoon Ginseng Powder

Directions:

1. Mix all ingredients together like you would a normal smoothie. Remember that adding more ice and milk will thicken it.

The Blueberries, ginseng, and flaxseed are great ways to naturally improve your concentration, and it's recommended that you take it early in the morning for the best results.

Drink #2 A Chocolate Delight

This is a smoothie that is also packed with everything you'd want for concentration issues, and the chocolate flavor helps to hide anything that tastes a little off. You make it like you would any other smoothie, and it's great for any time during the day.

Ingredients:

1. 2 Tablespoons Dark Cocoa Powder
2. 3 Tablespoons Honey
3. 8 Ounces Almond Milk, Frozen
4. 1 Banana, Frozen
5. ½ Cup Almond Butter
6. ½ Cup Spinach

Directions:

1. Start with the spinach and almond butter first, blending so that the spinach doesn't become stringy.
2. Add in all other ingredients, blending until smooth.

This smoothies is great because it provides you with a lot of the omega-3 fatty acids you need as well as B-vitamins to help.

Drink #3 A Green Tea Mixer

This is a hot or cold drink, depending on if you make it in advance and put it in the fridge. You will need to make it hot, not with cold water, if you want everything to steep properly. It's a type of tea, and it has a green tea base.

Ingredients:

1. 2 Tablespoons Green Tea Leaves
2. 1 Teaspoon Basil
3. 1 Teaspoon Rosemary
4. 1 Teaspoon Ginseng Powder
5. 3 Tablespoons Honey

Directions:

1. Boil water, placing in the green tea, basil, and rosemary. Reduce it to a simmer, letting the water simmer with the herbs in it for at least five minutes and up to ten.

2. Strain out the herbs, keeping the water warm. Add in honey and ginseng powder. Stir it completely.
3. Either let it cool or drink hot.

The rosemary, green tea, and basil and ginseng are all known to help with your focus. This is a tea that packs a powerful punch, and if you're drinking it hot you get an aromatherapy benefit from it as well due to the basil and rosemary. The honey is a natural sweetener.

Drink #4 A Sleepy Time Tea

If you're looking for something to help increase the quality and quantity of sleep you're getting as well as improve your focus for the next day, then this is the recipe for you. It's best when it's taken hot.

Ingredients:

1. 1 Teaspoon Passionflower
2. 2 Teaspoon Chamomile
3. 1 Teaspoon Ginseng Powder
4. ½ Teaspoon Lemon Balm
5. 2-3 Tablespoons Raw Honey

Directions:

1. Boil water, adding in all of the herbs as you reduce it to a simmer for five to ten minutes.

2. When the herbs are finished steeping, turn off the heat. Then, strain out all of the herbs.

3. Add honey to taste, and then drink while warm.

This is a tea that is packed with what you need to make sure that you're getting enough sleep and increasing your focus. You'll find that with the passionflower, lemon balm, and chamomile you're falling asleep instantly.

Drink #5 A Focusing Fruit Slush

This isn't exactly a smoothie, but it's a fruit flavored slush that will cool you down on any day. It's not as thick as a smoothie, so many people prefer it over them. Of course, if you want to make it into one, most people just add a quarter cup of vanilla or plain Greek yogurt.

Ingredients:

1. ¼ Cup Frozen Blueberries
2. ¼ Cup Shredded Kale
3. ¼ Cup Ice
4. ¼ Cup Frozen Raspberries
5. ½ Cup Frozen Orange Juice

Directions:

1. Just make sure to blend the kale and orange juice first.
2. Then, add in all the other ingredients. Add more ice if needed.

You can add honey to the mix if you need a sweetener, but you'll find that it's sweet on its own. There are many antioxidants and B-vitamins in this mix, but there is also vitamin C which as stated above is going to help your focus as well.

Drink #6 A Quick Focus

If you're looking for something that is going to increase your focus quickly and keep you awake instead of knocking you out, then this is the drink recipe for you.

Ingredients:

1. 1 Cup Green Tea, Frozen
2. 2 Tablespoons Dark Chocolate, Grated
3. 1 Teaspoon Rosemary Extract
4. ¼ Cup Almond Butter
5. 2 Tablespoons Honey
6. 1/3 Cup Frozen Papaya

Directions:

1. In this recipe, you can blend everything together. You don't have to worry about anything being too stringy. Having your fruit frozen and your green tea frozen is a great way to thicken it, but you can thicken it with ice as well.

Papaya also has B-vitamins, the dark chocolate and green tea are both a stimulant, the rosemary is a stimulant, and the almond butter is full of omega-3 fatty acids. All of these will help you with focus, and sweetening it with honey adds antioxidants that will helps as well.

Drink #7 A Green Smoothie

Leafy greens have already been proven to help with focus, and this smoothie recipe utilizes that knowledge. Of course, it adds in fruits that are sure to cover up the taste and make sure you feel like you're drinking a fruit smoothie despite the color.

Ingredients:

1. 1 Teaspoon Sunflower Seeds
2. 2 Teaspoons Flaxseed
3. ½ Cup Shredded Kale
4. ¼ Cup Baby Spinach

5. ½ Cup Almond Milk
6. ¼ Cup Blueberries, Frozen
7. ¼ Cup Papaya, Frozen

Directions:

1. Mix the kale, milk, and spinach together first.
2. Ground in the sunflower seeds and flaxseed.
3. Then add in your frozen fruit and ice if necessary, continuing to blend until it's at the thickness you desire.

The papaya and blueberries provides you with antioxidants and B-vitamins, you also get fiber and needed omega-3 fatty acids to help you. You can add honey to make sure that you have enough sweetener if needed.

Chapter 9. Final Tips to Keep in Mind

There are still a few final tips that you can keep in mind if you're looking to help increase your focus naturally. Better concentration is just right around the corner, but these tips will help you to speed the process along, achieving your goals a little faster and a little easier. These final tips will make focusing achievable, and it'll improve your attention span in the long term while still providing short term results.

Work When You Feel Comfortable:

This isn't a solution for everyone because you can't always choose your schedule but when you can, it'll work to your benefit. If you're comfortable in your environment, then you're

more likely to actually focus on what you're
doing. It'll help you to zone in. If you're in an
environment that makes you extremely
uncomfortable, then you're going to be
concentrating on what is making you
uncomfortable. This is one of the worst types of
distractions, and it's something you should try
to avoid whenever possible.

Don't Eat Heavy:

Eating healthy is going to help you with your
focus, especially if you're eating the right foods.
However, everyone knows that if you are eating
too heavy you are going to get too sleepy. So
avoid eating heavy when you have a lot of work
to do. It's going to distract you. So only eat
light, and try to work before any big meals
come up. If you're having an extremely hard
time focusing on a regular basis a juice fast or a
juice cleanse is actually recommended. Just

make sure to add in focus helpful fruits and vegetables if you do go on a juice cleanse or juice fast.

Exercise:

It is important that you are healthy if you want to have a healthy attention span and brain function as a whole. It's not enough to just eat right. You need to exercise fi you want your brain to work right in the first place. Exercising is also going to wake you up. It acts as a way to stimulate your body, and it helps to psych you up mentally, preparing you to focus on something for long periods of time. Exercise is great for you, and it's even better for your attention span.

Try a Power Nap:

If you're still having issues, you can always try a power nap, especially if you already know that you're not getting enough sleep or aren't on a regular sleep schedule. Try a power nap before you start if you want to get the most out of your work session. This is why children with ADD and ADHD are recommended to nap if they didn't sleep well the night before. It's a perfectly acceptable solution for adults who are suffering from a bad attention span as well. Before you lay down for your nap, remember to make sure all of your distractions are turned off, such as TV or music which would interrupt your sleep. If you don't, then you're not getting the most out of your nap.

Make it a No-Problem Zone:

Working in a no-problem zone is going to be the best way to make sure that you can maintain focus for a long period of time. For example, you're going to want to make sure that people aren't going to be barging in on you while you're trying to keep your attention on what you're trying to do. This is great if you have something particular that you're trying to accomplish.

Of course, you need to make sure that you limit your distractions as a whole anyways. You can be responsible for distracting yourself as well. This is because you can create an environment that is distracting. This is one reason that it is not recommended that you work in your bedroom. If you work in your bedroom, then you are more likely going to be distracted by your material items, such as your phone, TV, music player, or even the books that you have on the wall.

Space the Caffeine:

You've already learned that green tea and dark chocolate are a great way to help you focus because they both have caffeine, but don't over use it. You don't want to use too much caffeine or you're going to crash, and it won't help your attention span over the long term. Sometimes, it won't even help for the full day if you aren't careful. If you're having a hard time, take a cup of green tea and give it time to work, but don't continuously drink green tea and expect the same results. Remember that too much caffeine can cause you to get jittery and distracted, which will deter you from whatever you're trying to focus on.

Recognize a Pattern:

This one isn't as easy to do as it is to say. You need to recognize if you have a self-destructive pattern. If you have an issue concentrating regularly, you probably have a bad cycle that you've fallen into. You can't keep expecting different results by doing the same thing.

Before you can break the pattern, you need to actually recognize it though. So be careful, and analyze your actions. This is why having a to-do list and starting new habits is sure to help, but if you don't get rid of your old habits, then it'll only help so much. So the first step it to analyze. Then pick out the pattern that is detrimental, and then you'll be able to break the cycle. Of course, keep adding on better habits while you try to figure out where you're going wrong, and you're still going to increase your attention span in the meantime, helping you to be a more successful person.

Keep Plugging Away:

You're never going to gain a better attention span and start focusing better on a regular basis if you give up. Giving up is the rut that most people fall into. Never give up because there are many options out there for you to start concentrating a little better, and you can't give up even if you aren't getting the results that you want to through natural methods right away. A lot of vitamins and supplements work best when they've built up in your system, and not everyone is going to see results immediately from natural methods. Just keep trying, and you'll be able to find your way to a better attention span.

www.ingramcontent.com/pod-product-compliance
Lightning Source LLC
Chambersburg PA
CBHW061751050726

47598CB00002B/688